An Ocean's Autograph

Anjali Sahoo

Ukiyoto Publishing

All global publishing rights are held by

Ukiyoto Publishing

Published in 2023

Content Copyright © Anjali Sahoo

ISBN 9789359207285

www.ukiyoto.com

Dedication

To

My elder brother Ajit

(I call him "Bhai")

Who

Gave my poetry a direction,

For the first time

When I was struggling hard

To behold a rainbow

Behind a broken window sill!!

Thanks a ton for the

LIBRARY

He gifted!

Acknowledgement

I am highly grateful:

➢ To my parents for their constant psychological and moral support,

➢ To my spouse Dr. Sudhakar Sahoo for being with me all the time, both mentally and emotionally,

➢ To my son Anshu for his interest in reading whatever interests him,

➢ To my friends, colleagues, well wishers whoever said anything constructive and it meant a lot to me,

➢ To the renowned reviewers, publishers and readers of my poems for their genuine words of appreciation that help as a catalyst in my poetic journey,

➢ And lastly to the Great Divine Force for its graceful divine inspiration all the way through.

Foreword

A great poet doesn't try to be a great poet. By this, I mean that a poet writes because they are a poet and poetry is in them. It is not a craft learned in night school or taught by books (although even raw talent must be honed on the wheel of experience) but poetry is born of lived experience, of immersion in the smallest of things. Poetry is the gift of hearing melodies no one else can hear and seeing colours no one else can see… to look beyond the outward appearance of reality to its 'otherness', its inner soul. There is no place in poetry for pretence or grandstanding. Good poetry flows naturally like a river, bubbling up from its source in the mountains and flowing sombrely to the sea. It balances sincerity with style, cadence with meter… and sometimes it dispenses with meter altogether just for the hell of it. *Knowing when to break with convention is as important as knowing when to follow it.*Above all, a poem should say what it wants to say in the minimum number of words required to say it.

Anjali Sahoo is a poet who understands this. Reading one of Anjali's poems is to attend a masterclass in poetic economy. Her poems are often short but contain within them worlds of meaning, like little capsules which explode when ingested. She marvels at the 'surprise' of inspiration which seems to well up from some mysterious 'other' and the *pas de deux* between poet

and inspiration as the formless is woven into form,
as in *The Poet and the Poem,*

> *And suddenly echoing a soul's soul,*
> *The poem starts dancing*
> *With the poet,*
> *Before a music, soulful yet ceaseless,*
> *And the two remains no longer two*
> *But becomes one flesh,*
> *Before the universe starts synthesizing!*

and then there is *I Love to Write* in which the
author's joy in writing brims over in infectious
enthusiasm:

> *I love to write*
> *And I love to write,*
> *Since I know no other way*
> *Of skinning the words,*
> *Of veining the feelings,*
> *Of inuring the sensitivities,*
> *Of nerving the emotions*
> *Of blooding the thoughts*
> *And of poising a poem!*

while in *A Realisation,* she relives the moment she
understood that a great poem is one that
withstands the test of time,

> *The day I discerned that*
> *A single good poem,*
> *Even a single word*
> *Could be*
> *Eternally empowered enough*
> *To shield a poet*
> *From the gripping bite*

Of Time's
Grinding iron-like teeth!!

Something as simple as a spider's web, a spring wildflower, a rain drop, a grove of trees whispering, can spin off into a chain of associations. In *And*, a river experiences an existential crisis, finding the *'expiring ease'* of flowing sedately along through grassy meadows more convivial than losing its identity in the vast ocean, thus mirroring each person's dilemma in wanting to be a part of something greater but afraid of losing our identity in it, while in *Spider Web*, the web becomes a metaphor for the imprisoning of the mind under the authoritarian obsession with control:

> *The centre dictates and the edges follow*
> *The reason recedes and the wisdom fades*
> *The greatest lie in a hush-hush hollow*
> *And the least loudly march in parades,*

that final line *'the least loudly march'* vividly conjuring images of jack-booted soldiers goosestepping along some intimidating plaza while talentless careerists find their niche sucking up to Big Brother. In *The Smile*, a ray of sunlight piercing the darkness between trees becomes a living metaphor for how a simple smile can dissolve walls between people, and in *A Chorus Said*, the whispering of the trees becomes *"a table talk / between the saplings and Almighty God"* in which the trees bemoan their lack of limbs to rein in the depredations of humans, while in *The Brave Banyan*, the banyan tree becomes a symbol of struggle against climate change, storm and human development. Indeed, endurance is a key theme of Anjali Sahoo's poems, expressed in pieces such as *Life Is Just like a Moon*; *You Are You, My Child*; *My Mother*; *My Dear Self*; *Two Friends*; *Let Me*; *Red Fort*, etc. This is explicitly stated in *Life is Just like a Moon* where the metaphor of the Moon pulling on the earth is employed as an analogy for how the world tries to bend us to its will,

> *When situations seek even to pull an ocean,*
> *Resilience is vital*
> *Behind each calm and comely visage.*

It is a theme explored in *My Dear Self* which imagines Anjali in conversation with herself: "*Sometimes brokenness can also / Make a scaly sketch, / Having rough outlines of an evolution,*" and one can "*Live lovingly / Even in parts, pieces, particles and powder,*" and in *Monologue of Mr Mohanty* she tells us defiantly, "*I am none of your imagination / No bracket can limit my 'self'.*" Clearly, the author's mother served as an inspiration for survival, as in these lines from *My Mother*,

> *Her curly touch*
> *Turns everything gold*
> *May it be a day, a dream, a dahlia or dynamite!*
>
> *And on her hard times,*
> *When an Alps of agony*
> *Rests on her back,*
> *As loads of life,*
> *She starts becoming a dazzling piece of diamond,*

You need to be tough to be a mother! But however much the world breaks us into pieces, Anjali Sahoo reminds us, we can be pure and whole in the pieces, as in *You Are You, My Child,*

It's an interesting inversion: instead of being fragmentary parts in the bigger world, the world becomes just a part in us. The sentiment reminds me of a quote from Hemingway in *A Farewell to Arms* (1937): *"The world breaks everyone and afterward many are strong at the broken places."*

Anjali Sahoo is not one to be afraid of speaking out against poverty and exploitation as evinced in poems such as *Beneath, Hunger, A Dialogue,* and *She.* She deals with a particularly abhorrent episode: the December 2012 gang rape of Jyoti Singh, known as Nirbhaya (which translates as 'fearless') in Delhi, which prompted mass demonstrations at the time. Anjali Sahoo doesn't hold back in her praise for Nirbhaya's spirit and her contempt for the incidents of violence in her beloved India:

With a reference to the protest that followed the incident; note the barbed emphasis on "so-called". Elsewhere, Anjali finds herself in sympathy with exploited workers in *Beneath*, eulogizing hard work and noting that "*Almost all / Tends to totter beneath the weight of / A sweat droplet,*" and "*Fragility, too/ Sometimes / Becomes extremely enormous!!*" referring to the weight of a single additional maize grain being the straw that breaks the worker's back.

One of my favourite poems in the collection is *Rain on a Train*, one of her longest, but for me it is a standout poem in which a rain drop lands on the window of a train and begins sliding down towards the wheels. Only Anjali Sahoo could make us emote about the fate of a rain drop:

Still craving to find a little space of shelter
On my handkerchief,
And still longing for a huddle of togetherness,
At least once!

I won't spoil the ending! *Rain on a Train* demonstrates Anjali Sahoo's adept mastery of *pathetic fallacy*: the imbuing of inanimate nature with human emotions, a tradition dating back to the early nineteenth century Romantics such as Wordsworth and Coleridge and exemplified in Wordsworth's *The Prelude*. In *Storm*, Anjali envisages a storm as a mighty eagle swooping over towns and villages, whipping up air with its wings,

His bent beak and aware wings
With teeming tempo
Just moves on
Bulldozing and burying
Dreams half-done and half-dwelt!

while in *Whirlwind*, the cyclone is imagined as a stampeding horse kicking up dust with his hooves,

The whirlwind comes
At a gallop,
On a speeding horse's hoofs,
Madly sniffing and stamping
The inertia of the world around!

One of the personable things about Anjali Sahoo's poems is how she engages directly with the reader. She asks us questions, she interrogates us, she commands us to see.

Ah!
A legendary masterpiece
Is locally launched
Encircling the brown brow of
Rock-cut solidity,
With a coronet of quietude!

She says in *Ajanta and Ellora*, Buddhist cave monuments in Maharashtra, and

What would be the Time's denotation
Of God? Say…
After thousand years of duration
From today…

she asks in *A Man in a Temple*. The poem's counterpart, *A Girl in a Temple*, describes the protagonist's bewilderment as she stands in a line for the collection box and wonders what it has to do with God. The second half of the poem, however, absolutely brings the temple alive as though one were there:

Outside, a huge tree
Wears red ribbons,
Alas! A stone with incense sticks,
And on the boughs, the gibbons!
I spot the earthen lamps' flames merrily swing
And, a doll lamp in dreaminess is tied with a string!

One can smell the earth of the temple courtyard; see the glow of the lamps, the monkeys chattering in the trees. A feast of descriptive writing, indeed! The three poems *A Girl in a Temple*, *A Man in a Temple* and *Monologue of Mr Mohanty* showcase Anjali's mastery of *stream of consciousness* technique, allowing us insight into the protagonist's personal thoughts, as, for example, Mr Mohanty wondering,

> *"Who am I? Who am I?*
> *– A number, a word, or a chair?*
> *A fleeting fury, a snoozing silence,*
> *A discovery or despair!*

> *"Who am I? Who am I?*
> *–A tranquil tumult may be,*
> *Am I a monarch of my memories?*
> *And a serf of my sanity!"*

before coming to the conclusion that his 'self' is nothing one could ever imagine.

There is also a mischievous playfulness at work in Anjali Sahoo's poetry. In *Mammoth of My Dream*, she wonders what would happen if her dream of pet woolly mammoth stepped out of her imagination into the real world, and *Accident* is a delightful take on the phrase 'accident' waiting to happen' by imagining an accident as a provocateur lying in wait to catch people unawares,

> *I am a faceless dragon,*
> *In ambush,*
> *Quietly patting your path!*

> *I am a possibility –*
> *Anytime, anywhere,*
> *For anyone!*

Remember when reading this collection that with Anjali Sahoo, style never triumphs over substance but the two are perfectly interwoven, and the author's sincerity breathes through every line. So, I highly commend this volume of poems to you, the reader. May you take joy in reciting them to yourself (as indeed poetry is meant to be) and may you shed a tear occasionally like the little rain drop on the train.

Valentin Per Lind
Poet and reviewer, living in England
Author of *Corvix: Poems of Love, Loss and Death*

Preface

I WRITE

I write
Whenever I feel
A fresh fountainhead
Emanates
To
Evacuate its own self
From my inside,
Sometimes
With all its trickles,
Sometimes
With all its torrents!
###

Anjali Sahoo

Contents

Life Is Just Like A Moon

Life is just like a moon,

Waning and waxing,

Boating and floating,

Across the white and black clouds!

When situations seek even to pull an ocean,

Resilience is vital

Behind each calm and comely visage!

###

You Are You, My Child!

You are YOU, my child!

Whatever metal you are,

Be sure,

That's not mixed but pure and unique!

The world that shatters you everywhere

To be everybody,

Every now and then,

Just make that world your part!

###

Taj Mahal

Taj Mahal!!

I feel, it's a milk-washed beauty

Or a bubble of tear,

Or I feel it is a wonder of undying human spirit

Glowing upon the flame of time,

Or I feel it's a tribute

To the breathing memory of posterity,

Or possibly, it's an aroma

Intermingling with the essence of love,

Or I feel it's a sky's secret signature

Upon an earth's open ballot,

Or I feel it's an eternity

Wearing the robe of a snowy rhyme,

Or I feel nothing

But Taj Mahal is only taj mahal

And all that glitters is not always gold,

May be white diamond!!

###

My Mother

Her curly touch turns
Everything gold,
May it be a day, a dream, a dahlia or dynamite!

And on her hard times,
When an Alps of agony
Rests on her back,
As loads of life,
She starts becoming a dazzling piece of diamond,
Excelling
Even under the highest pressure!
###

Dream Big Dear!

Dream big dear!
For dream is a draft
Codifying Life's
Acts in fact!

Dream big dear!
For dream is a desk
With a rosy lamp
Sparkling grotesque!

Dream big dear!
For dream is a depot
Of fuels one fills
To keep a go!

Dream big dear!
For dream is a dome
Silvered with hope
When all is gone!
###

Ajanta And Ellora

Ah!
A legendary masterpiece
Is locally launched
Encircling the brown brow of
Rock-cut solidity,
With a coronet of quietude!

But, let me listen
The vivid voice
Of the meditative murals of ages,
That strives to discern
A silver synonym
For a history,
So poignantly patterned!
###

Red Fort

(After knowing about the historical plunder of Red
Fort)

A specimen of creativity

Still struggles

To salvage

His full-fledged figure!

His share of sorrow

Still strives

To shine

From sill to ceiling!

His walloping walls

Still scuffle

To suppress

The wild wounds

Set by some wanton weeds!

And after loads of loot, languish

And redness

Who says, longevity is his label!

###

Solitude

At times,
I feel cent percent fluent
With solitude,

Finding joy
In the simple things,

Savoring the flavor of each moment quietly,
Each experience calmly,

Testing the text and texture
Of an uncluttered life,

And above all restlessness,
Valuing space spaciously!
###

Spider Web

Let's watch the spider, spinning his web,
It's stretching and stretching, without waning
Things get trapped and tend to ebb
Losing own motion, mass and meaning!

The centre dictates and the edges follow
The reason recedes and the wisdom fades,
The greatest lie in a hush-hush hollow
And the least loudly march in parades!
###

Rain In Summer

Rain in summer starts
With a rhythmic fall of
Thousands of drops,
Making up dashing dance steps
In a sacred sequence
And stops all of a sudden,
Like a powerful prayer
Energizing each body, mind and soul!

###

Beneath

(Dedicated to all laborers on Labor Day)

Almost all

Tends to totter

Beneath the weight of

A sweat droplet,

May it be a

Mohenjo-Daro,

A Madurai,

A millennium,

A microcosm,

A matrix,

A milestone,

Or

A maize grain!

Fragility, too,

Sometimes

Becomes extremely enormous!!

###

Storm

The storm draws near
On eagle's clawed toes
To run a marathon
Over trees, towns and towers!

His bent beak and aware wings
With teeming tempo
Just moves on
Bulldozing and burying
Dreams half-done and half-dwelt!

Leaving a dim design of a
Topsy-turvy tranquility,
His yellow yet all-out eyes veer,
With a steady blinking
Of a thousand thunders!

###

I Wish I Had A World

I wish I had a world that I would say mine
With each bird and being, with each peony and pine!

I wish I had a world, where peace would hum
Over each panorama of power and pandemonium!

I wish I had a world, with dreams like a door
Would lie open for all, free and fair and more!

Each talent would grow with hallmark and hue
In a garden of gates, with fountains a few!

I wish I had a world, where love would beset
Like a shining weather, with a rainbow set!

I wish I had a world, where all needs would flush
Bliss would be a brook, with a perennial rush!

I wish I had a world, where all slayer arms,
Would creep in to an archive, with no set alarms!

I wish I had a world where disguise would not feign
Humanity would be the dynasty, over machine to
reign!

###

The Poet And The Poem

Before taking the form of a symphony
A poem seems to subsist in a muddle
Near a poet's parachute!

The poet looks back and front
In search of word-bird,
That casts a glance and goes away,
And revisits again to repay
A package on the porch of the planet
Named "poem"
Carried by the courier of conscience
Of the poet!

And suddenly echoing a soul's soul,
The poem starts dancing
With the poet,
Before a music, soulful yet ceaseless,
And the two remain no longer two

But become one flesh,

Before the universe starts synthesizing!

###

I Love To Write

I love to write
Without considering the answers of
Who, what, how,
When, where and why!

I love to write
Purely without longing for any
Trial, tempt or testimony!

I love to write and I love to write,
Since I know no other way
Of skinning the words,
Of veining the feelings,
Of inuring the sensitivities,
Of nerving the emotions,
Of blooding the thoughts,
And of poising a poem!

And of course,

That is no less fetching and fulfilling than

Bearing and rearing an infant

Out of dots, dashes and drops!

###

Whirlwind

The whirlwind comes
At a gallop,
On a speeding horse's hoofs,
Madly sniffing and stamping
The inertia of the world around!

It kicks and blows everything
With angry eyes and heated heels,
But escapes abruptly in the doldrums
With a melting momentum!!
###

Democracy, An Old Man

Since he laughs with lips open,

Do you think?

All is well,

He has a vault with elite gems,

But mostly to

Show and tell!

Since he talks with mouth open,

Is he happy?

A solitaire!

All owns him and he owns all,

But, within reach,

Who is where?

Since he sees with eyes open,

Are you sure?

He can see!

He has a conscience of grand size

But rarely to be

Used as key!

Morning Dew

The wintry morning

Drops in

On the whitish wings of dragonfly,

Rests a while

On the glistening grass,

And goes forth

Leaving mini silky-silvery orbs

Of beauty

Artistically liquefied,

To mirror the molecules of a million mirth!

###

Hunger

Each hunger has its haunted house,
Where a snake of fire crawls
There are windows with no eyes,
God is a rusty stuff on walls!

An illusion is the grey roof top
As humanity's shadow in a row,
The chimney hunts for bread or body,
May it be burnt or raw!

In the yard are broken scraps,
Is life collapsing near?
Beatitude bolted in the basement-
Death its name, seems dear!

###

Accident

I am a faceless dragon,
In ambush,
Quietly patting your path!

I am a possibility-
Anytime, anywhere,
For anyone!

Death's dagger
With a handle heavy with ivory
Casts a silvery glow
On all my darkness!

I love sucking blood,
Tearing flesh and
Smelling Life's wounded body,
That howls piercingly in pain!

You say,

I dwell in disloyalty,

But, I am destined to traverse your path

For a definitive cause,

When divinity dines with destiny

Inside a trackless tavern!

###

Fog

I behold grass tapping fog,
And goldenrods too,
I behold a cactus hugging fog,
And coral trees two!

Pampering a pure plenty,
Out of emptiness,
Fog only knows how to draw
Citadels of silence!

I Love Life

I love life in serenity sheer,
No rebuff there, no repulse dear!

I love life with all aloofness,
To offer a space of ease and grace!

I love life as a bud blooms blue,
So artless yet artful too!

I love life in lonesomeness,
Life seems mine and mirrors my face!

I love life in dream so sweet,
Life looks nonstop, new and neat!

I love life as much as a sky,
My eyes can't say it's how high!

But how life rolls across my poem!

Poem is life or life is a poem!!

###

Poem

A poem is a poem, a scented sandal wood,
A poem is a poem, with a hood within a hood!

A poem is a poem, in words, a feel is felt,
A thought fathers a sense; a baby of bliss is knelt!

A poem is a poem, a spotting of an atoll
Nowhere topographically, somewhere inside a soul!

A poem is a poem that cuts a death by lathe
A poem is a poem that lifts a life in depth!

A poem is a poem, like an ocean in a pot,
A poem is a poem, like a planet in a plot!

###

A Dialogue

The summer Sun in southern sky shone so high,

He sucked the Earth's juice, and slurped her dry,

Heated her like a pan without oil,

And covered a brown blanket, threw into turmoil,

But still the Earth was never-say-die,

In spite of all sweat, sob and sigh,

The tough Sun once asked loudly with mirth,

"How can you so far be living, Oh Earth?"

The Earth said, "I am sure, in a single flash,

You can burn and turn me into ash,

Can melt me, maul me and merge me well,

Can roll my body and toll my knell,

But above all, I am a mother in soul,

I endure and ensure my kids' needs all,

However, my motherhood mourns a lot,

When my garb like greeneries are cut,

My bosoms like hills are hollowed out,

My eyes like lakes are yellowed throughout,

My mouth like volcano and tummy like terrain,

My face like glacier and back like plain,

And my hair like valleys are rudely seized,

My limbs like rivers are bridged and squeezed,

You show your show- Who can barricade?

Let me die little grade by grade,

They will not die as long as I stay,

But who knows the sequel of my demise day?"

###

A Girl In A Temple

"Ding, ding, ding…
To two fat lips,
How madly the sweaty conch clings!

Oh, two queues inside,
Where to stand or stop?
Two coins, a single box,
Which one should I drop?

Oh! So tiresome the rattle!
Is it testing my mettle?
Does God follow the chatter?
Sorry! But, my tales are no doubt better.

Outside, a huge tree
Wears red ribbons,
Alas! A stone with incense sticks,
And on the boughs, the gibbons!
I spot the earthen lamps' flames merrily swing
And, a doll-lamp in dreaminess is tied with a string!"

###

A Man In A Temple

"What would be the Time's denotation
Of God? Say…
After thousand years of duration
From today,
I see, what else could He be?
And whatever couldn't be imagined now,
That else perhaps He would be!

But, did anyone hear my thought?
No way did I lead Him to naught."
###

A New Flower

A new sun
To newly adorn,
A new clock
To slowly turn,

A new dream
To plainly tap,
A new scheme to
To mainly map,

A new page
To gently start,
A new pen
To differently chart,

A new stone
To bowl away,
A new thorn
To roll away,

A new cloud
To lightly shuffle,
A new storm
To knightly tussle,

A new shower
To formally hail,
A new flower
To finally avail!

###

Monologue Of Mr. Mohanty

"Who am I? Who am I?
-A number, a word, or a chair?
A fleeting fury, a snoozing silence,
A discovery or despair!

"Who am I? Who am I?
-A tranquil tumult may be,
Am I a monarch of my memories?
And a serf of my sanity!

I am none of your imagination,
No bracket can limit my 'self'
I am a possibility, impossibility too,
Ever burgeoning- shelf by shelf!

Am I a grandstand with many seats?
While watching life's sport live,
And, I get my shoes, set my schedule,
While watching my 'self' drive?"
###

Rain On A Train

She is the raindrop,
With her unfurling awe,
Soothingly knocking
The closed window
Of my running train,

She is reciting the poem
Of the sky,
With perfect rhyme
And rhythm,

She is lifting her face
To peep into the berth
Perhaps to see
How far I am from her!

How striking her youthful blink,
And innocent stare are!

She is about to slip down

On the iron body
Of the train,
Slowly,
Silently,
Towards the roaring wheels below!

Still yearning for the warmness
Of my touch,
Still craving to find a little space of shelter
On my handkerchief,
And still longing for a huddle of togetherness,
At least once!

Oh, failing to hold,
She is breaking loose,
Feeling tired and
Almost lost,

Yes!
I could manage to hold her
On my ample palm,
At last once!
Thank God!!

A Chorus Said

A chorus said, "Give us human-like limbs, Oh Lord!
Nothing much is required to rein
Humans' mindless marathon on earth,
That roots the maladies of the universe in chain."

"Who is there?"- I stared through the grove,
But, everything grew so blurred and odd,
Was it nothing but just a table talk?
Between the saplings and Almighty God!
###

Soul Says

Soul says, "Hark at me Oh Body!
Here, dark is dense too much,
Please don't latch me any longer,
I am inside a hutch of clunch."

"Is it a Master's moan? Oh Lord!"
Says Body "but, it is so foreign!"
"Yes, it happens, dear!" says Soul,
"When a Supremo is not sovereign!"

Sometimes

Sometimes it's very great to think
About the great wanderers on earth,
Walking within the time's traffic,
Who become themselves- the preferred paths!

It's nothing but their deeds' decor,
That knit their names on shimmering star,
And, the world's to wink with warm wonder
And applause hour after hour!
###

One Day

One day I locked up my eyes with care,
And noticed with my soul's shine,
A sky with thousands of poems rare,
Trying to surf in ink-pot of mine!

The inkpot blew up over the north,
Ink just sprang up from dark hole,
And each dot turned a word of worth,
A poised poem became a cosmos whole!

###

And

And subsequently
The river realized that
A rover's life
Of expiring ease,
Having no
Preset
Tour itinerary,
Local tenancy
Or neighborhood was
More fulfilling,
Than the risk of
Dropping
Each second,
Each atom of the soul,
Inside a topsy-turvy
Oceanic extravaganza
And
Finally
Connecting to a

Devouring disconnectedness
Forever!

###

She

(Dedicated to all NIRBHAYAAS)

She was a

Flaming fire ball,

The one who swallowed the hottest fire

Of a wind-blown mob forest,

Vehemently burning

The grandest humanity to ashes,

In a small bowl

Of her purified soul,

And spreading over the

So-called civilized land

An immovable cloud of black smoke!!

###

Remarkably

Remarkably,
There is so much to reflect on,
When a tidal wave
Makes a mockery of
An algae-glossed-rock,
For her green grin,
Masking
His own pivotal role
Behind the black curtain
Of a new-moon-night!
###

A Realization

Leaf-shoots

Started to sprout

On my soul's soil

And sweepingly grew dense,

The day I discerned that

A single good poem,

Even a single word

Could be

Eternally empowered enough

To shield a poet

From the gripping bite

Of Time's

Grinding iron-like teeth!!

###

My Dear Self

"My dear self, Are you broken today?"

"Yes!"

"But, do you know,
You are not a looking glass,
Once broken, hence gone forever?"

"Ok! But…"

"Sometimes brokenness can also
Make a scaly sketch,
Having rough outlines of an evolution"

"Really?"

"Yes, it's true, when you love
To live lovingly
Even in parts, pieces, particles and powder!"
###

A Name That Matters

Delhi is Delhi and Rome is Rome,
With own spring, with own storm,
With own mask, with own grin,
In each name, a world does spin.

With all quirks, with all traits,
Names loll and leap on dates,
With own make, with own mold,
Zinc is Zinc and Gold is Gold.

A Thought

One day

When a poem will bother a poet

With a quick question,

Who is more crucial -A poem or a poet?

The poet will say a poet

Rather listlessly

Without any forethought,

And the poem will abruptly

Elope with "someone" in anguish,

Not realizing that

A poet is none without his poem,

And nothing more than

Everything in a poem

Is a poet's plenty

And

That "someone" with her

Is none other than

The poet himself!

###

Remember

Remember
Even a burning Sun
Can have a dent
In darkness,
And to delete a dent,
You can never
Burn an entire sky down!
###

Two Friends

"Dear friend, are you listening to me?"

"What?"

"I feel a weird weightiness
In the hub of my heart…"

"Yes, sometimes,
Nothing seems weightier than
Your moving memories…"

"Ok! But, I feel like
Leaving and losing
A large part of my own self somewhere else…"

"But bear in mind friend,
Regardless of what
You stick together of your self
Or what you split apart,

You are still intact!"

"Really?"

"Yes, and I observe,
The blossom of your better self is still swaying
In the breeze
Beneath a brighter sky"!

"True!"

"Please trust me, dear,
Above all,
I'm your friend!"
###

Let Me

May it be
East, west, north or south,
Let me take a trip into
Myself first!

Let me cure
What is crazy in me!

Let me fix
What is fractured in me!

Let me wrap up
What is outspread in me!

Let me discern
What is displaced in me!

Let me lubricate
What is rusted in me!

Let me rerun
What is defunct in me!

Let me remodel
What is collapsed in me!

Let me wake up
What is asleep in me!

Let me pile up
What is plucked in me!

Let me replant
What is uprooted in me!

Let me dispose of
What is debris in me!

Let me finally fan
What is fragrant in me!

And let me flow forth alone
Like a clapping cascade

With silvery pure water!

I have no longing
To blend in a flock,
However flamboyant it may be!
###

Who Said?

"Like a well-fed weed
Footless yet in full speed,
The "I" in you swings high."
I sensed,
Who said?
And
Why?
After a while
A soul's sunny smile,
I found in a wild weed's eye.

###

While Writing A Poem

While writing a poem,

This evening,

I wondered,

Words crawled slowly towards me

Like tiny toddlers,

Like my pens were their Doctor's Kits,

Like my paper weight was a ride-on toy for them,

Like my books were their decorative pillows,

Like my study table was a welcoming carrom board,

Like my library was a carpeted playroom

With colorful walls,

Made just for them,

And like they had previously played there

For years together!

###

How A Poet Feels

It is almost impossible to explain
How a poet feels
After writing a poem,
How an echo of delight escalates up to the sky,
How an unvoiced code starts cracking,
How life's remainder starts reflecting
The rays of readiness to be,
How a shrinking space swells slowly in small parts,
How pieces of sunshine jump
Towards a covert world,
That's just born with a faint blush
Creeping over his fair face…

And, it is almost impossible to explain
How a poet feels
After writing a poem!

The Smile

The forest is mutely mystic,
Dark for half a mile,
A racy ray pushes a teak,
Like a sparkling smile:

Like that, a smile though short,
Shelled yet pearly when seen,
Pushes a wall to naught,
That stands tall in between!
###

A Question

If I could dare to

Put Almighty God

Only one probing question,

Then,

That would certainly be:

"Oh God, why is man made

To rest in floral peace,

Only after a tender thunder like death,

That too,

When life is found fully

Unlaced,

Unzipped

And

Unbuckled?"

###

In A Moment Of All Blankness

In a moment

Of

All blankness,

Beyond the boundaries of

Past memories

Or

Present melodies,

Oh Dear!

There is lush greenery,

Let's meet there,

Where

The shadows of our souls,

Too

Start greening themselves,

Pulling all weeds out

From an unsealed- "You and I"!

###

A Little Girl Asked Me

A little girl asked me,
Am I now leading a life of my childhood choice?
I failed to reply her instantly
In a single word as
Her query started melting my so-called state of being
Then and there:

I think if I am 100% honest
To myself,
This is not the best version of me,
That has elevated to the frequency and wavelength
Of
My childhood dream,
I think I have not yet tracked me out
In the midst of the night moon, stars and comets,
I think my waiting for
Something extra-ordinary
To occur everyday
Has not yet been fulfilled,

I think I have not yet measured

The heavenly heartbeat

Of the anonymous wild flowers

And their eminent butterflies-friends,

I have not yet reached to the soulful point

Where the royal rainbow

Bows down to touch the feet of the earth,

I have not yet multiplied a grain of sand

To stop the deluge of rain water

And to make a pool

For my playful paper boats,

I think I have not yet molded

From malleable clay,

A sculpt shape

Of

That unknown mysterious entity,

Who is Parent of the man on earth!

###

It Never Bothers Me

It never bothers me,

How far I sail,

To which port

I am bound,

It never bothers me,

From what fairyland

I hail,

And which fort

Rings me round.

It never bothers me,

How long icy wind blows,

To which realm

Waves run, why?

It never bothers me,

Why the helm wheel slows,

And which hymn

He hums, why?

###

The Mammoth Of My Dream

Let me cuddle

The mammoth

Of my dream,

Let me cradle his

Curved tusk,

Let him be a riddle

Or an unbelief

Now to deem,

But what if

Once he appeared

And

The world was thunder struck!

###

Bit By Bit

Step by step

And

Bit by bit,

Deeds decide

Our

Peak, pitch and pit!

###

Trees Are Just Like Priced Tickets

Trees are just like priced tickets,

To admit us

To the Earth's

Day and night shows,

Without which

None can even dream to enter,

And here

The difference is:

The tickets themselves stand for

Years together,

To facilitate the entry

Of audience

Into this round auditorium!

###

Adequate Enough

Today,

My tear seems

As intense as a torrent,

And

As engulfing as a

Sea Wave,

Slowly but surely

Becoming

Adequate enough to

Immerse me

Underneath!

###

I Puffed Up A Bunch Of Balloons

I puffed up a bunch of balloons

That went up

To reach the blues,

Carrying everything

My soul longed for,

All that, all my life

I had been making my move to,

With a wish

To

Keep that ever in one piece

Inside the closet of the stars,

Above all the stuff of unsettledness

Of this seemingly unremitting world of ours;

What if

Lightning flashed and thunder boomed on their way,

Or

The balloons got caught in a tall tree,

With a slice of a dark night

And

Some pieces of black clouds inside,

Then!

###

It May Be Easy

It may be easy to spot

A Moon

In someone's eyes,

Even when

She moves through a horrifying hurricane

Inside her heroic heart,

But

It is simply difficult to

Dig through her heart's dotted debris

That accumulates

At the bottom,

In a shuttered silence!

###

Tide Of Joy

Tide of joy,
Don't lift me more,
Just roll in to
My memory shore,

That is full of
Sorrow sand dunes,
And some inflated
Bubbly balloons!
###

Dear World!

Dear world!
Don't be in a hurry
All the time!

Let me sense every breathe
You breathe,
Every sound you whisper,
In an agreeable
Slowness
And
Silence!

I doubt,
You often wheeze and
Feel tightness
In your chest,

Am I right?
###

Flaw

I found a flaw in me,
Like a black mole, see!
I leant on it with care,
It dissolved one day there!

I found a flaw in me,
And greeted mutely in glee,
It grew and got so tough,
Like rash and redness rough!

###

The Brave Banyan

In the end,

The brave banyan,

Too,

Fell down,

Losing grasp on his

Entwined fingers, arms and legs

With soil,

No matter how he

Shrank and stretched,

How he defied and disentangled,

And how he built himself

To the highest specification,

To become

Both brutal and brittle

In the same ratio,

Only to survive

And

Not to succumb to

The torturous tornado

Of

Time!

###

A Spring Wild Flower

A spring wild flower
With two tiny leaves
Along the stem,
Just entered into my room
Through the window,
And
Surprisingly,
Touched the soul
Of
My soul,
With her
Curved fingers,
Leaving me in light
That
God's architecture was there at a standstill
And
That could be owned
At the cost of
Nothing

But

Pure love only!

###

Don't Bottle Up

Don't bottle up your dreams,

Dear!

Don't aim to box up your soul's spectrum

As saw dust in a carton,

Just give it its abundant sky

And see

How a vivid rainbow

Constitutes its form,

When the light of your deed and dedication

Passes through

The prism of your life!

###

Had I Not

Had I not drawn a circle around me

With all its boundlessness,

Had I not had my cottage,

My cluster of trees,

With shades of Bakul, Siris and Karanj,

My zinnias and jasmines,

My little stream and its pebbles,

My grassy bank with hopping grasshoppers,

My moths and lady bugs,

And

My pond and puddles,

I would have possibly expired

Too early

In some defined editions

Of

Barriers and boundaries!

###

Just Decide

"My world ends here "He said.
"It's ok" She replied,
"But, don't collapse into a heap,
Just decide to make the ending point
Your point of view,
To view
Your grandest sky,
Your roundest moon
And
Your fondest rainbow,
Of which
Once upon a time,
You were the gladdest architect!"
###

How Rare You Are!

(A tribute to poet Jayanta Mahapatra)

The sun glows

But

Heat is low,

The wind blows

But

Speed is slow,

The fire burns

But

No fierce glare,

All mourns,

Just

How rare you are!

###

About the Author

Anjali Sahoo

With over a decade of writing poems in English, Anjali Sahoo has a uniquely original voice that shines through in her newest poetry book An Ocean's Autograph. Like her two other poetry books, i.e. A Tryst with Thunder (2021) and Soliloquy of Eternity (2023), the present book too, contributes to the direction of Indian wit, intelligence, and philosophy, presenting to our thoughts a trustworthy portrayal of us and of all mankind. Without regard for anybody else's guidelines, she follows her own path, and the end result is a work with exceptional strength and authenticity. Anjali's love of Indian subjects, her feeling of directness and economy in the use and choice of words with the use of alliteration, her peculiar blending of traditional meters and modern words, as well as her monologues and dialogues, were all on display in her first two volumes. That trend simply continues even in her third volume: An

Ocean's Autograph. Though Anjali had started writing in her mother tongue, i.e. Odia much earlier, she has spent the last two decades reading and writing English poetry, giving her creative reflections a palpable spark!